contents

Z, Canada, US and
K readers
ease note that Australian
up and spoon measurements
e metric. A conversion chart
opears on page 63.

chocolate hazelnut croissants

2 sheets ready-rolled puff pastry
⅓ cup (110g) chocolate-hazelnut spread
30g dark eating chocolate, grated finely
25g butter, melted
1 tablespoon icing sugar

1 Preheat oven to hot (220°C/200°C fan-forced). Lightly grease two oven trays.

2 Cut pastry sheets diagonally to make four triangles. Spread triangles with chocolate-hazelnut spread, leaving a 1cm border; sprinkle each evenly with chocolate.

3 Roll triangles, starting at one wide end; tuck tips under and curve ends in slightly to form crescent shape. Place 3cm apart on trays; brush croissants with melted butter.

4 Bake, uncovered, about 12 minutes or until croissants are browned lightly. Serve croissants, warm or at room temperature, lightly dusted with sifted icing sugar.

preparation time 15 minutes
cooking time 15 minutes
makes 8
per croissant 17.7g total fat (8.8g saturated fat); 1154kJ (276 cal); 26.6g carbohydrate; 3.4g protein; 0.8g fibre

scrambled eggs with chorizo

250g chorizo, sliced thickly
8 eggs
¾ cup (180ml) cream
2 tablespoons coarsely chopped fresh chives
10g butter

1 Cook chorizo, in batches, on heated grill plate (or grill or barbecue) until browned both sides; cover to keep warm.
2 Break eggs into medium bowl, whisk lightly; whisk in cream and half of the chives.
3 Melt butter in medium frying pan over low heat; cook egg mixture, stirring, until egg just begins to set.
4 Serve scrambled eggs, sprinkled with remaining chives, with chorizo on slices of the toasted bread of your choice.

preparation time 5 minutes
cooking time 10 minutes
serves 4
per serving 51g total fat (24.4g saturated fat); 2378kJ (569 cal); 3.3g carbohydrate; 26.4g protein; 0.3g fibre

french toast with berry compote

4 eggs
½ cup (125ml) cream
¼ cup (60ml) milk
1 teaspoon finely
   grated orange rind
1 teaspoon ground
   cinnamon
¼ cup (90g) honey
100g butter, melted
8 thick slices sourdough
   bread (560g)
¼ cup (40g) icing sugar
berry compote
1 teaspoon cornflour
⅓ cup (80ml) water
2 cups (300g) frozen
   mixed berries
2 tablespoons
   caster sugar
1 tablespoon finely
   grated orange rind

1 Make berry compote.
2 Break eggs into medium bowl, whisk lightly; whisk in cream, milk, rind, cinnamon and honey.
3 Heat about a quarter of the butter in medium frying pan. Dip 2 bread slices into egg mixture one at a time; cook, uncovered, until browned both sides. Remove from pan; cover to keep warm. Repeat with remaining butter, bread slices and egg mixture.
4 Sprinkle french toast with sifted icing sugar; serve with warm berry compote.

berry compote Blend cornflour with the water in small saucepan until smooth; add remaining ingredients. Cook until mixture almost boils and thickens slightly.

preparation time 15 minutes
cooking time 10 minutes
serves 4
per serving 42.1g total fat (24.8g saturated fat); 3106kJ (743 cal); 77.7g carbohydrate; 16.2g protein; 5.5g fibre
tip Do not use wheaten cornflour, as this will make the berry compote appear cloudy. Use maize (corn) cornflour, instead.

pancetta and eggs

8 slices pancetta (120g)
2 green onions, chopped coarsely
4 eggs
4 thick slices white bread, toasted

1 Preheat oven to moderately hot (200°C/180°C fan-forced).
Grease four holes of 12-hole (⅓-cup/80ml) muffin pan.
2 Line each of the holes with 2 slices of the pancetta,
overlapping to form a cup shape. Divide onion among
pancetta cups; break 1 egg into each cup.
3 Bake, uncovered, about 10 minutes or until eggs are
just cooked and pancetta is crisp around edges. Remove
from pan carefully. Serve on toast.

preparation time 10 minutes
cooking time 10 minutes
serves 4
per serving 10.1g total fat (3.3g saturated fat); 844kJ
(202 cal); 13.1g carbohydrate; 14.9g protein; 0.9g fibre

honey-roasted muesli

¾ cup (60g) rolled oats
½ cup (55g) rolled rye
½ cup (55g) rolled rice
¼ cup (15g) unprocessed wheat bran
½ cup (175g) honey
1 tablespoon vegetable oil
⅓ cup (35g) coarsely chopped walnuts
¼ cup (35g) pepitas
1 teaspoon ground cinnamon
⅓ cup (50g) coarsely chopped dried apricots
⅓ cup (20g) coarsely chopped dried apples
¼ cup (35g) raisins

1 Preheat oven to moderate (180°C/160°C fan forced).
2 Combine oats, rye, rice and bran in medium baking dish; drizzle evenly with honey and oil. Roast, uncovered, 5 minutes. Stir; roast, uncovered, further 10 minutes.
3 Remove from oven; stir in remaining ingredients. Serve with milk or yogurt.

preparation time 10 minutes
cooking time 15 minutes
serves 4
per serving 19.8g total fat (1.8g saturated fat); 2178kJ (521 cal); 74g carbohydrate; 8.3g protein; 12.7g fibre
tip You can double or triple the quantity of the ingredients and store the muesli in an airtight container in the refrigerator for up to three months.

blueberry bircher muesli

2 cups (180g) rolled oats
1 cup (250ml) fresh orange juice
250g yogurt
¼ cup (90g) honey
½ cup (125ml) milk
1 large green apple (200g), grated coarsely
120g fresh blueberries
¾ cup (75g) walnuts, roasted, chopped coarsely

1 Combine oats, juice, yogurt, honey and milk in large bowl; stand 30 minutes or overnight.
2 Stir in apple. Serve topped with blueberries and walnuts.

preparation time 15 minutes (plus standing time)
serves 4
per serving 20.3g total fat (3.7g saturated fat); 2027kJ (485 cal); 63.7g carbohydrate; 12.2g protein; 5.7g fibre

baked ricottas with roasted tomatoes

2 tablespoons olive oil
2 cloves garlic, crushed
¼ cup (40g) pine nuts
150g baby spinach leaves, chopped coarsely
2 medium tomatoes (380g)
400g ricotta cheese
2 eggs, beaten lightly
⅔ cup (50g) finely grated parmesan cheese
2 tablespoons finely chopped fresh chives

1 Preheat oven to hot (220°C/200°C fan forced). Grease four holes of six-hole (¾-cup/180ml) texas muffin pan.
2 Heat half of the oil in medium frying pan; cook garlic and nuts over low heat, stirring constantly, until nuts start to brown lightly. Add spinach; cook, covered, about 2 minutes or until spinach wilts. Uncover; cook 2 minutes or until liquid evaporates. Remove from heat.
3 Cut each tomato into eight wedges; place in medium baking dish, drizzle with remaining oil. Roast, uncovered, 20 minutes.
4 Meanwhile, combine ricotta, egg, parmesan and chives in large bowl with spinach mixture. Divide mixture among pan holes.
5 Bake, uncovered, about 20 minutes or until ricottas are firm. Serve baked ricottas with roasted tomatoes.

preparation time 10 minutes
cooking time 25 minutes
serves 4
per serving 34.3g total fat (12.3g saturated fat); 1710kJ (409 cal); 4g carbohydrate; 21.9g protein; 3g fibre

cheesy chips topped with bacon and sour cream

1kg frozen potato chips
1 tablespoon vegetable oil
1 clove garlic, crushed
6 bacon rashers (420g), sliced thinly
1½ cups (180g) coarsely grated cheddar cheese
½ cup (120g) sour cream
1 tablespoon finely chopped fresh chives
1 fresh small red thai chilli, seeded, chopped finely

1 Preheat oven to moderately hot (200°C/180°C fan forced). Lightly grease oven tray.
2 Place chips, in single layer, on tray; cook, uncovered, about 20 minutes or until brown.
3 Meanwhile, heat oil in medium frying pan; cook garlic and bacon, stirring, until bacon is crisp. Drain on absorbent paper.
4 Place chips on ovenproof serving platter. Sprinkle with bacon mixture and cheese; cook, uncovered, in oven about 5 minutes or until cheese melts.
5 Meanwhile, combine sour cream, chives and chilli in small bowl.
6 Serve chips topped with sour cream mixture.

preparation time 10 minutes
cooking time 25 minutes
serves 4
per serving 51.4g total fat (22.1g saturated fat); 3256kJ (779 cal); 49.5g carbohydrate; 30.7g protein; 2.8g fibre

mediterranean vegetables and haloumi bruschetta

1 small french breadstick
1 tablespoon olive oil
1 small eggplant (230g), sliced thinly
200g haloumi cheese, sliced thinly
2 tablespoons plain flour
2 medium egg tomatoes (150g), sliced thinly
2 tablespoons fresh baby basil leaves
1 tablespoon drained, rinsed baby capers

1 Preheat oven to hot (220°C/200°C fan forced).
2 Cut bread, on an angle, into eight slices; brush both sides with half of the oil, place on oven tray. Bake, uncovered, about 5 minutes.
3 Meanwhile, cook eggplant on heated oiled grill plate (or grill or barbecue) until just tender.
4 Coat haloumi in flour, shake away excess; cook on heated oiled grill plate (or grill or barbecue) until browned lightly.
5 Divide eggplant, haloumi, tomato, basil and capers evenly among bruschetta. Drizzle with remaining oil.

preparation time 15 minutes
cooking time 10 minutes
serves 4
per serving 14.6g total fat (6.3g saturated fat); 1204kJ (288 cal); 24.2g carbohydrate; 15.1g protein; 3.3g fibre

chicken sang choy bow

You need about two medium butter lettuce for this recipe.

4 dried shiitake mushrooms
1 tablespoon peanut oil
1kg chicken mince
4cm piece fresh ginger (20g), chopped finely
1 clove garlic, crushed
227g can water chestnuts, drained, chopped coarsely
227g can sliced bamboo shoots, drained, chopped coarsely
¼ cup (60ml) hoisin sauce
¼ cup (60ml) oyster sauce
2 tablespoons soy sauce
2 tablespoons cornflour
½ cup (125ml) chicken stock
3 cups (240g) bean sprouts
4 green onions, sliced thickly
18 large butter lettuce leaves

1 Place mushrooms in small heatproof bowl, cover with boiling water; stand 20 minutes, drain. Discard stems; chop mushroom caps finely.
2 Heat oil in wok; stir-fry chicken, ginger and garlic until chicken is just changed in colour.
3 Add mushrooms, water chestnuts, bamboo shoots, sauces and blended cornflour and stock to chicken; stir-fry until mixture boils and thickens. Stir in sprouts and onion.
4 Divide lettuce leaves among serving plates; spoon sang choy bow into lettuce leaves.

preparation time 10 minutes (plus standing time)
cooking time 15 minutes
serves 6
per serving 17.7g total fat (4.7g saturated fat); 1513kJ (362 cal); 15.4g carbohydrate; 35.4g protein; 4.6g fibre

noodle and vegetable rolls

60g rice vermicelli
noodles
½ medium carrot (60g),
grated coarsely
½ small chinese
cabbage (350g),
shredded finely
1 tablespoon fish sauce
1 tablespoon
brown sugar
¼ cup (60ml)
lemon juice
12 x 17cm-square
rice paper sheets
12 large fresh
mint leaves
sweet chilli
dipping sauce
¼ cup (60ml) sweet
chilli sauce
1 tablespoon fish sauce
1 tablespoon lime juice

1 Place noodles in medium heatproof bowl, cover with boiling water; stand until just tender, drain. Using kitchen scissors, cut noodles into random lengths.
2 Place noodles in medium bowl with carrot, cabbage, sauce, sugar and juice; toss gently to combine.
3 To assemble rolls, place 1 sheet of rice paper in medium bowl of warm water until just softened. Lift sheet from water carefully; place, with one point of the square sheet facing you, on board covered with tea towel. Place a little of the vegetable filling and one mint leaf vertically along centre of sheet; fold top and bottom corners over filling then roll sheet from side to side to enclose filling. Repeat with remaining rice paper sheets, vegetable filling and mint leaves.
4 Combine ingredients for sweet chilli dipping sauce in small bowl.
5 Serve rolls with sweet chilli dipping sauce.

preparation time 20 minutes
cooking time 5 minutes
makes 12 rolls
per roll 0.2g total fat (0g saturated fat); 188kJ (45 cal); 9g carbohydrate; 1.4g protein; 0.8g fibre
per tablespoon dipping sauce 0.4g total fat (0.1g saturated fat); 71kJ (17 cal); 2.7g carbohydrate; 0.4g protein; 0.6g fibre

stuffed chicken breast with spinach salad

4 single chicken breast fillets (800g)
80g cheddar cheese, sliced thinly
4 slices bottled char-grilled red capsicum (170g)
100g baby spinach leaves
2 tablespoons olive oil
1 tablespoon lemon juice
1 small red onion (100g), sliced thinly

1 Using tip of small knife, slit a pocket in one side of each chicken fillet, taking care not to cut all the way through. Divide cheese, capsicum and a few spinach leaves among pockets; secure with toothpicks.
2 Cook chicken on heated oiled grill plate, uncovered, until cooked through. Cover chicken; stand 10 minutes. Remove toothpicks; slice thickly.
3 Meanwhile, make the spinach salad by combining oil, juice, onion and remaining spinach; toss gently to combine.
4 Serve chicken with salad.

preparation time 10 minutes
cooking time 20 minutes
serves 4
per serving 22.9g total fat (6.9g saturated fat); 1672kJ (400 cal); 3.5g carbohydrate; 45g protein; 1g fibre

fish with herb and tomato dressing

We used blue eye in this recipe, but you can use any firm white fish, such as perch or ling.

12 baby new potatoes (480g), halved
4 medium zucchini (480g), quartered
2 tablespoons olive oil
4 white fish fillets (800g)
2 medium egg tomatoes (150g), chopped finely
2 tablespoons lemon juice
1 tablespoon finely chopped fresh dill
2 tablespoons finely chopped fresh basil

1 Boil, steam or microwave potato and zucchini, separately, until tender; drain.
2 Meanwhile, heat half of the oil in large non-stick frying pan; cook fish until cooked through. Remove from pan; cover to keep warm.
3 Heat remaining oil in same cleaned pan; cook tomato and juice, stirring, 2 minutes. Remove from heat; stir in herbs.
4 Divide fish and vegetables among serving plates; top with tomato mixture.

preparation time 15 minutes
cooking time 15 minutes
serves 4
per serving 10.8g total fat (1.5g saturated fat); 1371kJ (328 cal); 18.5g carbohydrate; 38.1g protein; 4.6g fibre

garlic and sage lamb racks with roasted red onion

3 large red onions (900g)
⅓ cup (80ml) olive oil
2 tablespoons coarsely chopped fresh sage
4 cloves garlic, chopped coarsely
4 x 4 frenched-trimmed lamb cutlet racks (600g)

1 Preheat oven to hot (220°C/200°C fan forced).
2 Halve onions then slice into thin wedges; place in large baking dish with half of the oil.
3 Combine remaining oil in small bowl with sage and garlic. Using hands, press sage mixture all over lamb; place lamb on onion.
4 Roast, uncovered, about 25 minutes or until lamb is browned all over and cooked as desired. Cover with foil; stand 10 minutes.

preparation time 10 minutes
cooking time 25 minutes
serves 4
per serving 44.1g total fat (14.4g saturated fat); 2404kJ (575 cal); 12.4g carbohydrate; 33.5g protein; 3.4g fibre

beef and asparagus stir-fry

1 tablespoon rice vinegar
1 tablespoon soy sauce
1 tablespoon dry sherry
2 cloves garlic, crushed
750g beef strips
2 tablespoons peanut oil
2 medium brown onions (300g), sliced thickly
500g asparagus, trimmed, halved
1 teaspoon cornflour
2 tablespoons oyster sauce
1 tablespoon black bean sauce
⅓ cup (80ml) beef stock

1 Combine vinegar, soy sauce, sherry and garlic in large bowl; add beef, toss to coat in mixture.
2 Heat half of the oil in wok; stir-fry beef, in batches, until browned.
3 Heat remaining oil in wok; stir-fry onion and asparagus until onion just softens.
4 Return beef to wok with blended cornflour, oyster sauce, black bean sauce and stock; stir-fry until mixture boils and thickens slightly.

preparation time 10 minutes
cooking time 15 minutes
serves 4
per serving 16.4g total fat (4.7g saturated fat); 1501kJ (359 cal); 6.9g carbohydrate; 44.4g protein; 2.4g fibre

eggplant, fetta and capsicum stack with mesclun salad

2 medium red
    capsicums (400g)
¼ cup (60ml) olive oil
2 tablespoons
    lemon juice
1 clove garlic, crushed
1 large eggplant (500g)
1 cup (150g) drained
    sun-dried tomatoes,
    chopped coarsely
¼ cup (40g) seeded
    kalamata olives,
    chopped coarsely
½ cup loosely packed
    fresh basil leaves, torn
100g mesclun
2 tablespoons
    red wine vinegar
200g fetta cheese,
    cut into 8 slices
1 tablespoon small
    whole fresh basil
    leaves, extra

1 Quarter capsicums; discard seeds and membranes. Cook capsicum on heated oiled grill plate, skin-side down, until skin blisters and blackens. Cover with plastic wrap 5 minutes; peel away skin.

2 Meanwhile, combine 2 tablespoons of the oil in small bowl with juice and garlic. Cut eggplant lengthways into eight slices, brush slices both sides with oil mixture; cook on heated oiled grill plate, uncovered, brushing occasionally with oil mixture, until just tender.

3 Combine tomato, olives and torn basil in small bowl. Place mesclun in medium bowl, drizzle with vinegar and remaining oil; toss gently to combine.

4 Place 1 slice of the eggplant on each serving plate; top each with 2 slices of the cheese, 2 pieces of the capsicum and another eggplant slice. Top with tomato mixture, sprinkle with extra basil leaves; serve with salad.

preparation time 15 minutes
cooking time 15 minutes
serves 4
per serving 27.8g total fat (17.8g saturated fat); 1718kJ (411 cal); 23.3g carbohydrate; 16.4g protein; 10.3g fibre

marinated vegetable pasta

*Rigatoni is a ridged pasta that looks like thick, short penne;
its grooves and wide centre help hold chunky sauces.*

2 cloves garlic, crushed
290g jar mixed antipasto, drained, chopped coarsely
340g jar marinated artichokes, drained, quartered
⅔ cup (160ml) chicken stock
700g bottled tomato pasta sauce
500g rigatoni pasta
½ cup coarsely chopped fresh basil
50g parmesan cheese, shaved

1 Heat garlic, antipasto and artichoke in large frying pan,
stirring, 3 minutes. Stir in stock and sauce; bring to a boil.
Reduce heat; simmer, uncovered, about 5 minutes or until
sauce thickens slightly.
2 Meanwhile, cook pasta in large saucepan of boiling
water, uncovered, until just tender; drain.
3 Add pasta and basil to sauce; toss gently to combine.
Divide pasta among serving bowls; top with cheese.

preparation time 10 minutes
cooking time 15 minutes
serves 4
per serving 9.1g total fat (3.5g saturated fat); 2671kJ
(639 cal); 111.8g carbohydrate; 25.5g protein; 10.8g fibre

spaghettini with parsley basil pesto

1 cup firmly packed fresh basil leaves
1 cup firmly packed fresh flat-leaf parsley leaves
2 tablespoons toasted pine nuts
2 cloves garlic, quartered
2 tablespoons finely grated pecorino cheese
½ cup (125ml) olive oil
375g spaghettini pasta

1 Blend or process herbs, nuts, garlic and cheese until combined. With the motor operating, gradually add half of the oil in thin, steady stream; process until combined.
2 Meanwhile, cook pasta in large saucepan of boiling water, uncovered, until just tender; drain.
3 Combine pasta, pesto and the remaining oil in large saucepan; toss gently to combine.

preparation time 10 minutes
cooking time 10 minutes
serves 4
per serving 35.2g total fat (4.8g saturated fat); 2608kJ (624 cal); 64.7g carbohydrate; 12.5g protein; 4.8g fibre

white chocolate and honeycomb mousse

2 eggs, separated
250g white eating chocolate, chopped coarsely
1 tablespoon caster sugar
1 teaspoon gelatine
⅓ cup (80ml) milk
300ml thickened cream
2 x Violet Crumble Bars, chopped coarsely

1 Place egg yolks, chocolate, sugar, gelatine and milk in small heavy-based saucepan; stir continuously, over low heat, until mixture is smooth. Transfer mixture to large bowl; cool.
2 Beat egg whites in small bowl with electric mixer until soft peaks form.
3 Beat cream, in separate small bowl, with electric mixer until soft peaks form.
4 Fold cream and honeycomb into chocolate mixture then fold in egg whites. Divide mixture among four 1-cup (250ml) glasses; refrigerate mousse, covered, 4 hours before serving.

preparation time 10 minutes
(plus cooling and refrigeration time)
cooking time 5 minutes
serves 4
per serving 55.8g total fat (36.2g saturated fat); 3210kJ (768 cal); 59.5g carbohydrate; 11.4g protein; 0.1g fibre
tip Care must be taken when heating the white chocolate mixture; if the heat is too high, the chocolate will "seize", that is, it will become clumpy, grainy and, therefore, unusable.

brownie ice-cream stacks
with hot fudge sauce

500ml vanilla ice-cream
80g butter
150g dark eating chocolate,
  chopped coarsely
¾ cup (165g) firmly packed
  brown sugar
2 eggs, beaten lightly
½ cup (75g) plain flour
¼ cup (60g) sour cream
½ cup (55g) coarsely
  chopped walnuts
hot fudge sauce
50g dark eating chocolate,
  chopped coarsely
½ cup (125ml) cream
2 tablespoons brown sugar
½ teaspoon instant
  coffee granules

1 Line base and sides of 8cm x 26cm bar cake pan with baking paper. Spoon ice-cream into medium bowl, stand 10 minutes to soften slightly. Press ice-cream into pan, cover with foil; freeze overnight.

2 Preheat oven to moderate (180°C/160°C fan-forced). Line base and sides of another 8cm x 26cm bar cake pan with baking paper.

3 Combine butter and chocolate in small saucepan; stir over low heat until mixture is smooth. Transfer chocolate mixture to medium bowl. Stir in sugar; cool.

4 Stir egg then flour, sour cream and nuts into chocolate mixture. Spread mixture into pan. Bake, uncovered, about 40 minutes.

5 Cool brownie in pan. Turn onto wire rack; remove lining paper. Trim narrow ends; cut into 12 slices.

6 Meanwhile, make hot fudge sauce.

7 Turn ice-cream out of pan; cut into eight slices. Stack alternate slices of ice-cream and brownie, starting and finishing with brownie. Drizzle each stack with hot fudge sauce.

hot fudge sauce Combine ingredients in small saucepan; stir over low heat until mixture is smooth. Bring to a boil, reduce heat; simmer, uncovered, 2 minutes.

preparation time 20 minutes (plus freezing time)
cooking time 45 minutes
serves 4
per serving 68.4g total fat (38g saturated fat); 4389kJ (1050 cal); 101.7g carbohydrate; 13.1g protein; 2.1g fibre

choc crunch ice-cream with strawberries

1 litre vanilla ice-cream
8 Tim Tam biscuits, chopped coarsely
250g fresh strawberries, halved

1 Spoon ice-cream into medium bowl, stand 10 minutes to soften slightly.
2 Fold through biscuits until just combined. Return ice-cream to container, cover; freeze until firm.
3 Serve ice-cream with strawberries.

preparation time 10 minutes (plus freezing time)
serves 4
per serving 39.2g total fat (25.3g saturated fat); 2909kJ (696 cal); 78.8g carbohydrate; 10.7g protein; 1.9g fibre

apple and brown sugar crumbles

5 medium green apples (750g)
2 tablespoons lemon juice
1 tablespoon brown sugar
¼ teaspoon mixed spice
brown sugar crumble
½ cup (75g) plain flour
80g butter, chopped
⅓ cup (75g) firmly packed brown sugar
¼ teaspoon mixed spice

1 Preheat oven to moderately hot (200°C/180°C fan-forced). Lightly grease four 1-cup (250ml) ovenproof dishes; place on oven tray.
2 Peel and core apples; chop coarsely. Combine apple, juice, sugar and spice in medium bowl.
3 Make brown sugar crumble.
4 Divide apple mixture among dishes (pile apple high as it shrinks during cooking). Press brown sugar crumble on top of apples.
5 Bake about 30 minutes or until browned.
6 Serve hot with ice-cream or cream, if desired.
brown sugar crumble Place flour in medium bowl; rub in butter until combined. Add sugar and spice; mix well.

preparation time 10 minutes
cooking time 30 minutes
serves 4
per serving 16.9g total fat (10.8g saturated fat); 1593kJ (381 cal); 56.5g carbohydrate; 2.9g protein; 4.2g fibre

caramel pear self-saucing puddings

425g can pear slices in natural juice, drained
¾ cup (110g) self-raising flour
⅓ cup (75g) firmly packed brown sugar
20g butter, melted
⅓ cup (80ml) milk
⅓ cup (40g) pecans, chopped coarsely
2 tablespoons icing sugar
caramel sauce
½ cup (110g) firmly packed brown sugar
¾ cup (180ml) boiling water
50g butter, chopped

1 Preheat oven to moderate (180°C/160°C fan forced). Grease four shallow 1¼-cup (310ml) ovenproof dishes; place on an oven tray.
2 Divide pear slices among dishes.
3 Combine flour, sugar, butter and milk in small bowl; mix well. Spread mixture evenly over pear slices. Sprinkle with nuts.
4 Make caramel sauce.
5 Pour caramel sauce slowly over the back of a spoon over mixture in dishes.
6 Bake about 25 minutes or until firm.
7 Sprinkle with sifted icing sugar; serve immediately with cream or ice-cream, if desired.

caramel sauce Combine ingredients in medium heatproof jug; stir until sugar is dissolved and butter is melted.

preparation time 15 minutes
cooking time 25 minutes
serves 4
per serving 22.7g total fat (10.5g saturated fat); 2178kJ (521 cal); 77.5g carbohydrate; 4.9g protein; 2.9g fibre

passionfruit coconut tart

You need about six passionfruit for this recipe.

1 cup (80g) desiccated coconut
¾ cup (165g) caster sugar
½ cup (75g) plain flour
4 eggs, beaten lightly
1⅓ cups (330ml) milk
125g butter, melted
½ cup (125ml) passionfruit pulp
1 tablespoon lemon juice
2 tablespoons icing sugar

1 Preheat oven to moderate (180°C/160°C fan-forced). Grease 24cm pie dish.
2 Combine coconut, sugar and flour in large jug; stir in combined egg, milk, butter, pulp and juice.
3 Pour mixture into dish. Bake, uncovered, about 1 hour or until set; cool in dish. Serve tart dusted with sifted icing sugar.

preparation time 15 minutes
cooking time 45 minutes
serves 8
per serving 24.5g total fat (16.8g saturated fat); 1584kJ (379 cal); 34g carbohydrate; 7g protein; 4.2g fibre

nashi galette

Galette is a French term for a flat tart that can be round or rectangular, sweet or savoury. You can use either pear or apple, or a combination of both, instead of the nashi.

2 sheets ready-rolled
   puff pastry
3 medium nashi (600g)
½ teaspoon finely
   grated lime rind
⅓ cup (80ml) lime juice
⅓ cup (80ml) water
½ cup (110g) caster sugar
30g butter, melted
1 tablespoon brown sugar

1 Preheat oven to hot (220°C/200°C fan-forced). Lightly grease two oven trays.

2 Cut pastry sheets in half; place two halves on each oven tray. Fold in long sides of each pastry piece about 2cm; press folded sections lightly then turn short ends in, making three small folds in each.

3 Cut whole unpeeled nashi into 1cm slices. Discard small end slices; you need 16 similar-size nashi rounds for this recipe.

4 Combine rind, juice, the water and caster sugar in large heavy-based frying pan; stir over high heat, without boiling, until sugar is dissolved. Bring to a boil, add nashi to syrup, in batches if necessary; cook over low heat about 10 minutes or until just tender. Remove nashi from syrup with a slotted spoon; cool slightly. Reserve syrup in pan.

5 Place nashi slices on pastry pieces; brush with combined melted butter and brown sugar.

6 Bake, uncovered, about 20 minutes or until browned lightly.

7 Meanwhile, boil reserved syrup about 10 minutes or until reduced to a thick glaze; brush hot galettes with glaze.

preparation time 15 minutes
cooking time 1 hour 15 minutes
serves 4
per serving 25.4g total fat (14.3g saturated fat); 2429kJ (581 cal); 84.2g carbohydrate; 5.7g protein; 4.4g fibre

almond and strawberry friands

6 egg whites
185g butter, melted
1 cup (120g) almond meal
1½ cups (240g) icing sugar
½ cup (75g) plain flour
100g strawberries, sliced thinly
2 tablespoons icing sugar, extra

1 Preheat oven to moderately hot (200°C/180°C fan-forced). Grease 12 ½-cup (125ml) rectangular or oval friand pans, stand on oven tray.

2 Place egg whites in medium bowl; whisk lightly with a fork until combined. Add butter, almond meal, icing sugar and flour to bowl; using wooden spoon, stir until just combined. Divide mixture among pans; top with strawberry slices.

3 Bake friands about 25 minutes. Stand friands in pans 5 minutes then turn, top-side up, onto wire rack to cool. Serve warm, or at room temperature, dusted with extra sifted icing sugar.

preparation time 20 minutes
cooking time 25 minutes
makes 12
per friand 18.5g total fat (8.7g saturated fat); 1204kJ (288 cal); 27.1g carbohydrate; 4.8g protein; 1.3g fibre

flourless hazelnut chocolate cake

⅓ cup (35g) cocoa powder
⅓ cup (80ml) hot water
150g dark eating chocolate, melted
150g butter, melted
1⅓ cups (295g) firmly packed brown sugar
1 cup (100g) hazelnut meal
4 eggs, separated
1 tablespoon cocoa powder, extra

1 Preheat oven to moderate (180°C/160°C fan-forced).
Grease deep 19cm-square cake pan; line base and sides
with baking paper.
2 Blend cocoa with the water in large bowl until smooth.
Stir in chocolate, butter, sugar, hazelnut meal and egg yolks.
3 Beat egg whites in small bowl with electric mixer until
soft peaks form; fold into chocolate mixture in two batches.
4 Pour mixture into pan; bake about 1 hour or until firm.
Stand cake 15 minutes, then turn cake, top-side up, onto
wire rack to cool. Dust with sifted extra cocoa to serve.

preparation time 20 minutes (plus standing time)
cooking time 1 hour
serves 9
per serving 29.9g total fat (13.3g saturated fat); 1898kJ
(454 cal); 42g carbohydrate; 7g protein; 1.9g fibre
tips This cake can be made up to four days ahead and
refrigerated, covered. It can also be frozen for up to three
months. Hazelnut meal replaces the flour in this recipe.

pear and almond cake
with passionfruit glaze

*You will need about
four passionfruit for
this recipe.*

185g butter, chopped
½ cup (110g)
  caster sugar
3 eggs
1½ cups (180g)
  almond meal
¼ cup (35g) plain flour
420g can pear halves in
  natural juice, drained
passionfruit glaze
⅓ cup (80ml)
  passionfruit pulp
⅓ cup (80ml)
  light corn syrup
1 tablespoon
  caster sugar

1 Make passionfruit glaze.
2 Preheat oven to moderately slow (170°C/150°C fan-forced). Grease 22cm springform tin; line base and side with baking paper.
3 Beat butter and sugar in medium bowl with electric mixer until light and fluffy. Add eggs, one at a time, beating until combined between each addition. Stir in almond meal and flour.
4 Spread mixture into pan; top with pear halves. Bake about 50 minutes. Stand cake 5 minutes, then turn cake, top-side up, onto wire rack. Pour passionfruit glaze over cake.
passionfruit glaze Stir ingredients in small saucepan over heat, without boiling, until sugar dissolves. Bring to a boil; reduce heat. Simmer, uncovered, without stirring, about 2 minutes or until thickened slightly; cool.

preparation time 30 minutes
cooking time 50 minutes
serves 10
per serving 27g total fat (11.2g saturated fat); 1563kJ (374 cal); 27.7g carbohydrate; 6.5g protein; 3.3g fibre
tip The cake and glaze can be made a day ahead; refrigerate, covered separately, until required.

mango coconut cake

250g butter, softened
1 teaspoon
coconut essence
1½ cups (330g)
caster sugar
4 eggs
⅔ cup (160ml)
mango puree
2 cups (160g)
desiccated coconut
2½ cups (375g)
self-raising flour
coconut frosting
1 egg white
1¼ cups (200g)
icing sugar
2 teaspoons
mango puree
¾ cup (60g)
desiccated coconut

1 Preheat oven to moderate (180°C/160°C fan-forced). Grease deep 22cm-round cake pan; line base with baking paper.
2 Make coconut frosting.
3 Beat butter, essence and sugar in small bowl with electric mixer until combined; do not over beat. Add eggs, one at a time, beating only until combined between additions.
4 Transfer mixture to large bowl. Using wooden spoon, stir in puree and coconut, then flour. Spread mixture into pan.
5 Bake about 1¼ hours. Stand cake 5 minutes then turn cake, top-side up, onto wire rack to cool. Spread top of cold cake with coconut frosting.
coconut frosting Beat egg white in small bowl with electric mixer until foamy. Gradually beat in icing sugar, 1 tablespoon at a time. Using fork, mix in puree and coconut. Cover frosting with plastic wrap until required, pressing plastic directly onto surface of frosting.

preparation time 35 minutes
cooking time 1 hour 15 minutes (plus cooling time)
serves 12
per serving 32.5g total fat (23.6g saturated fat); 2454kJ (587 cal); 69.5g carbohydrate; 7.1g protein; 4.4g fibre
tips You can buy frozen pureed mango at most supermarkets, or you can puree the flesh of a fresh mango (you need a mango weighing about 450g). Mango nectar can be substituted, but the flavour will not be as intense.
Cake will keep for up to two days stored in an airtight container.

glossary

almond meal also known as ground almonds.

bacon rashers also known as slices of bacon.

bamboo shoots the tender shoots of bamboo plants, available in cans; drain and rinse before use.

bean sprouts also known as bean shoots; tender new growths of assorted beans and seeds germinated for consumption as sprouts.

black bean sauce a chinese sauce made from fermented soy beans, spices, water and wheat flour.

butter use salted or unsalted (sweet) butter; 125g is equal to 1 stick butter.

capers the grey-green buds of a shrub, sold either dried and salted or pickled in a vinegar brine; tiny young ones, called baby capers, are also available.

capsicum also known as bell pepper or, simply, pepper. Discard membranes and seeds before use.

cheese

cheddar the most common cow-milk 'tasty' cheese; should be aged, hard and have a pronounced bite.

fetta a crumbly textured goat or sheep-milk cheese with a sharp, salty taste.

haloumi a cream-coloured, firm, sheep-milk cheese matured in brine; has a minty, salty fetta flavour.

parmesan also known as parmigiano; a hard, grainy cow-milk cheese. The curd is salted in brine before being aged for up to two years.

pecorino is the generic Italian name for cheeses made from sheep milk. It's a hard, white to pale yellow cheese. Pecorino is usually matured for eight to 12 months.

ricotta a soft white cow-milk cheese with a sweet, moist taste and a slightly grainy texture; roughly translates as "cooked again". It's made from whey, a by-product of other cheese making, to which fresh milk and acid are added.

chilli available in many different types and sizes. Use rubber gloves when seeding and chopping fresh chillies as they can burn your skin. Removing seeds and membranes lessens the heat level.

sweet chilli sauce the comparatively mild, thai sauce made from red chillies, sugar, garlic and vinegar; used as a condiment more often than in cooking.

thai small, medium hot, and bright red in colour.

chinese cabbage also known as peking or napa cabbage, wong bok or petsai. Elongated in shape with pale green, crinkly leaves.

chorizo a sausage of Spanish origin, made of coarsely ground pork and highly seasoned with garlic and chilli.

cocoa powder also known as cocoa; the unsweetened cocoa beans are dried, roasted then ground.

cornflour also known as cornstarch; used as a thickening agent in cooking.

desiccated coconut dried and finely shredded coconut.

eggplant also known as aubergine.

eggs some recipes in this book call for raw or barely cooked eggs; exercise caution if there is a salmonella problem in your area.

fish sauce called naam pla on the label if it is Thai made; the Vietnamese version, nuoc naam, is almost identical. Made from pulverised salted fermented fish (most often anchovies); has a pungent smell and strong taste. There are many versions of varying intensity, so use according to your taste.

flour

plain an all-purpose flour made from wheat.

self-raising plain flour sifted with baking powder in the proportion of 1 cup flour to 2 teaspoons baking powder.

gelatine we used powdered gelatine; it is also available in sheet form known as leaf gelatine.

ginger also known as green or root ginger; the thick gnarled root of a tropical plant. Can be kept, peeled, covered with dry sherry in a jar and refrigerated, or frozen in an airtight container.

hazelnut meal also known as ground hazelnuts.

hoisin sauce a sweet-spicy, thick chinese paste.

light corn syrup made from cornstarch; an imported product available in some supermarkets, delicatessens and health food stores.

mesclun a salad mix of assorted young lettuce and other green leaves.

mince also known as ground meat, as in beef, pork, lamb, veal and chicken.

mixed spice a blend of ground spices usually consisting of cinnamon, allspice and nutmeg.

mushrooms

button small, cultivated white mushrooms having a delicate, subtle flavour.

caps slightly larger and with a stronger flavour than buttons, caps, sometimes called cups, are firm textured and ideal for soups, pies and casseroles.

field the correct name for mushrooms found growing wild on forest floors.

flat large, flat mushrooms with a rich earthy flavour; ideal for filling and barbecuing.

oyster grey-white mushroom shaped like a fan, also known as abalone. Prized for their smooth texture and subtle, oyster-like flavour.

shiitake when fresh are also known as chinese black, forest or golden oak mushrooms; although cultivated, they have the earthiness and taste of wild mushrooms. Are large and meaty; often used as a substitute for meat in some Asian vegetarian dishes. When dried, they are known as donko or dried chinese mushrooms; rehydrate before use.

swiss brown light to dark brown mushrooms with full-bodied flavour also known as roman or cremini.

nashi also called japanese or asian pear; a member of the pear family but similar in appearance to an apple.

noodles, vermicelli also known as sen mee, mei fun or bee hoon. Before using, soak the dried noodles in hot water until they're soft (about 15 minutes), then boil them briefly (from 1 to 3 minutes) and rinse with hot water.

nutella a sweet chocolate hazelnut spread.

oil

olive made from ripened olives. *Extra virgin* and *virgin* are the first and second press, respectively, of the olives and are therefore considered the best. *Extra light* and *light* refers to the taste and not the fat levels.

peanut pressed from ground peanuts; most commonly used oil in Asian cooking because of its high smoke point (capacity to handle high heat without burning).

vegetable any of a number of oils sourced from plants rather than animal fats.

onion

green also known as scallion or, incorrectly, shallot; an immature onion picked before the bulb has formed.

red also known as spanish, red spanish or bermuda onion; a sweet-flavoured, large, purple-red onion.

oyster sauce Asian in origin, this rich, brown sauce is made from oysters and their brine, cooked with salt and soy sauce, and thickened with starches.

pancetta cured pork belly; if unavailable, bacon can be substituted.

pepitas dried pumpkin seeds.

pine nuts also known as pignoli; not in fact a nut but a small, cream-coloured kernel from pine cones.

raisins dried sweet grapes.

ready-rolled puff pastry packaged sheets of frozen puff pastry, available from supermarkets.

rice paper sheets also known as banh trang. Made from rice paste and stamped into rounds or squares.

rice vinegar a colourless vinegar made from fermented rice and flavoured with sugar and salt. Sherry can be substituted, if preferred.

rolled rice flattened rice grain rolled into flakes and similar in appearance to rolled oats.

rolled rye flattened rye grain rolled into flakes and similar in appearance to rolled oats.

soy sauce also known as sieu, is made from fermented soy beans.

spinach also known as english spinach and, incorrectly, silver beet.

sugar

brown an extremely soft, fine granulated sugar retaining molasses for its characteristic colour and flavour.

caster also known as superfine or finely granulated table sugar.

icing also known as confectioners' or powdered sugar; granulated sugar crushed with cornflour.

water chestnuts have a crisp, white, nutty-tasting flesh. Best eaten fresh, however, canned are more easily available.

index

conversion chart

MEASURES

One Australian metric measuring cup holds approximately 250ml, one Australian metric tablespoon holds 20ml, one Australian metric teaspoon holds 5ml.

The difference between one country's measuring cups and another's is within a two- or three-teaspoon variance, and will not affect your cooking results. North America, New Zealand and the United Kingdom use a 15ml tablespoon.

All cup and spoon measurements are level. The most accurate way of measuring dry ingredients is to weigh them. When measuring liquids, use a clear glass or plastic jug with the metric markings.

We use large eggs with an average weight of 60g.

DRY MEASURES

METRIC	IMPERIAL
15g	½oz
30g	1oz
60g	2oz
90g	3oz
125g	4oz (¼lb)
155g	5oz
185g	6oz
220g	7oz
250g	8oz (½lb)
280g	9oz
315g	10oz
345g	11oz
375g	12oz (¾lb)
410g	13oz
440g	14oz
470g	15oz
500g	16oz (1lb)
750g	24oz (1½lb)
1kg	32oz (2lb)

LIQUID MEASURES

METRIC	IMPERIAL
30ml	1 fluid oz
60ml	2 fluid oz
100ml	3 fluid oz
125ml	4 fluid oz
150ml	5 fluid oz (¼ pint/1 gill)
190ml	6 fluid oz
250ml	8 fluid oz
300ml	10 fluid oz (½ pint)
500ml	16 fluid oz
600ml	20 fluid oz (1 pint)
1000ml (1 litre)	1¾ pints

LENGTH MEASURES

METRIC	IMPERIAL
3mm	⅛in
6mm	¼in
1cm	½in
2cm	¾in
2.5cm	1in
5cm	2in
6cm	2½in
8cm	3in
10cm	4in
13cm	5in
15cm	6in
18cm	7in
20cm	8in
23cm	9in
25cm	10in
28cm	11in
30cm	12in (1ft)

OVEN TEMPERATURES

These oven temperatures are only a guide for conventional ovens.
For fan-forced ovens, check the manufacturer's manual.

	°C (CELSIUS)	°F (FAHRENHEIT)	GAS MARK
Very slow	120	250	½
Slow	150	275 – 300	1 – 2
Moderately slow	170	325	3
Moderate	180	350 – 375	4 – 5
Moderately hot	200	400	6
Hot	220	425 – 450	7 – 8
Very hot	240	475	9

Are you missing some of the world's favourite cookbooks

The Australian Women's Weekly cookbooks are available from bookshops, cookshops, supermarkets and other stores all over the world. You can also buy direct from the publisher, using the order form below.

MINI SERIES £3.50 190x138MM 64 PAGES

TITLE	QTY	TITLE	QTY	TITLE	QTY
4 Fast Ingredients		Drinks		Party Food	
15-minute Feasts		Fast Fish		Pasta	
30-minute Meals		Fast Food for Friends		Pickles and Chutneys	
50 Fast Chicken Fillets		Fast Soup		Potatoes	
After-work Stir-fries		Finger Food		Risotto	
Barbecue		Gluten-free Cooking		Roast	
Barbecue Chicken		Healthy Everyday Food 4 Kids		Salads	
Barbecued Seafood		Ice-creams & Sorbets		Simple Slices	
Biscuits, Brownies & Biscotti		Indian Cooking		Simply Seafood	
Bites		Indonesian Favourites		Skinny Food	
Bowl Food		Italian		Stir-fries	
Burgers, Rösti & Fritters		Italian Favourites		Summer Salads	
Cafe Cakes		Jams & Jellies		Tapas, Antipasto & Mezze	
Cafe Food		Kids Party Food		Thai Cooking	
Casseroles		Last-minute Meals		Thai Favourites	
Char-grills & Barbecues		Lebanese Cooking		The Fast Egg	
Cheesecakes, Pavlova & Trifles		Low Fat Fast		The Packed Lunch	
Chinese Favourites		Malaysian Favourites		Vegetarian	
Chocolate Cakes		Mince Favourites		Vegetarian Stir-fries	
Christmas Cakes & Puddings		Mince		Vegie Main Meals	
Cocktails		Muffins		Wok	
Crumbles & Bakes		Noodles		Young Chef	
Curries		Outdoor Eating		TOTAL COST	£

Photocopy and complete coupon below

Name _____

Address _____

_____ Postcode _____

Country _____ Phone (business hours) _____

Email*(optional) _____

* By including your email address, you consent to receipt of any email regarding this magazine, and other emails which inform you of ACP's other publications, products, services and events, and to promote third party goods and services you may be interested in.

I enclose my cheque/money order for £ _____ or please charge £ _____

to my: ☐ Access ☐ Mastercard ☐ Visa ☐ Diners Club
PLEASE NOTE: WE DO NOT ACCEPT SWITCH OR ELECTRON CARDS

Card number | | | | | | | | | | | | | | | | | |

3 digit security code *(found on reverse of card)* _____

Cardholder's signature _____ Expiry date ____ /____

To order: Mail or fax – photocopy or complete the order form above, and send your credit card details or cheque payable to: Australian Consolidated Press (UK), Moulton Park Business Centre, Red House Road, Moulton Park, Northampton NN3 6AQ, phone (+44) (01) 604 497531, fax (+44) (01) 604 497533, e-mail books@acpmedia.co.uk. Or order online at www.acpuk.com
Non-UK residents: We accept the credit cards listed on the coupon, or cheques, drafts or International Money Orders payable in sterling and drawn on a UK bank. Credit card charges are at the exchange rate current at the time of payment.
All pricing current at time of going to press and subject to change/availability.
Postage and packing UK: Add £1.00 per order plus 25p per book.
Postage and packing overseas: Add £2.00 per order plus 50p per book. **Offer ends 31.12.2007**